D0116025

The Way of Peace

A New System of Spiritual Guidance

Paul Ferrini

Book Design
by Paul Ferrini and Lisa Carta
Thanks to Don Stewart for Copy Editing

Library of Congress Catalog Card Number: 99-90727
ISBN 1-879159-42-2

Manufactured in the United States of America

HEART WAYS
PRESS

P.O. Box 99
Greenfield, MA 01302

The Way of Peace

This book contains the inspirational words of Jesus, which I have received over the last few years. I have arranged these words into an oracle—a method of spiritual guidance—to help you connect with your inner Christ Nature. Open the book spontaneously to any page whenever you need some assistance in perceiving a situation in your life more peacefully. Or learn the simple divinatory procedure described below so that you can receive responses to specific questions that you have. You will be amazed at the depth and accuracy of the answers you receive.

The Way of Peace is designed to provide you with spiritual guidance for the variety of challenges you face in everyday life. The 216 readings in this book were culled from the four books in my *Christ Mind* series: *Love Without Conditions, The Silence of the Heart, Miracle of Love* and *Return to the Garden.* If you want to explore this material further, you are referred to these books, as well as to the two compilations of this material entitled *Reflections of the Christ Mind* and *I am the Door*. (See the back section of this book for more information about ordering these books).

It is my hope that this little book will bring you to the peace, joy and wisdom that lie in your heart and in the quiet places of your mind.

Paul Ferrini

The Way of Peace as an Oracle

Following the procedure described below will help you frame your question, relax into a receptive state of consciousness, and perform the divinatory process in the most effective way, thus ensuring an appropriate response to your question.

First, find a quiet time when you can devote at least ten to fifteen minutes to the process. Begin by taking some deep breaths and closing your eyes. Bring your awareness to the present moment. Breathe and relax for several minutes. Performing the divinatory procedure in a hurried manner will not yield accurate results.

Once you are relaxed, begin to frame your question. Keep it as simple as possible. Here are some examples of good questions:

What do I need to look at to improve my relationship with my husband?

Is it for my highest good to leave this job at this time?

What is the underlying reason why I am having such a difficult time with _____?

Once you have framed the question to your satisfaction, empty your mind of past thoughts and be open to receiving a new perspective on your situation. Pray for a response that will guide you to the best thinking and course of action available to you. Holding the dice cupped in your hands, let your energy flow into the dice until there is a resonant field around them. Then shake the dice for at least fifteen seconds and throw all three dice onto a flat surface in front of you.

Write down the numbers you get for the blue die, the purple die, and the green die and consult tables 1 and 2 to determine the number of your divinatory response. Then, turn to that number in this book.

Read through the response and notice any intuitive connections you make as you are reading. These connections are important and should be written down. Then, re-read the response and consider it in the context of your question.

There may be times when the title of the reading (or one sentence within the reading) seems more responsive to your question than the reading as a whole. A flood of insights may be evoked even by a single word or phrase. In this case, the oracle is primarily functioning as trigger for your own inner wisdom. Remember, the process of divination is a partnership between the oracle and you. Often, your intuitive connections provide the necessary link between your question and the oracular response to it.

Once you have considered the response fully, write down your reflections in a special divination journal and make sure to include the question asked and the date of the query. You may find that you learn a great deal about yourself by reading your journal entries over a specific period of time.

The Way of Peace should be consulted one time only on a given question, and never more than once per day. If you do not understand or approve of the response you receive to your question, live with the question and the response for a few days. Then, if necessary, you can reframe your question and ask again.

The more energy you put into preparing a safe, relaxed, meditative space for consulting the oracle, the more accurate your divinatory response is likely to be. To put it simply, you will get out of the process what you put into it. You are advised to approach each consultation as a sacred ritual and to ask the oracle only those questions that come from the depths of your heart.

Finding Your Divinatory Response

TABLE 1

PURPLE DIE

	1	2	3	4	5	6
1	1	2	3	4	5	6
2	7	8	9	10	11	12
3	13	14	15	16	17	18
4	19	20	21	22	23	24
5	25	26	27	28	29	30
6	31	32	33	34	35	36

(Left label: BLUE DIE)

TABLE 2

1	0 + BASE #
2	36 + BASE #
3	72 + BASE #
4	108 + BASE #
5	144 + BASE #
6	180 + BASE #

(Left label: GREEN DIE)

1. Find the number you rolled on the blue die on the left side of Table 1.

2. Find the number you rolled on the purple die on the top of Table 1.

3. Look across the row chosen by the blue die in #1 above and down the column chosen by the purple die in #2 above until the row and column intersect. This square will give you your base number. *For example, if the blue die is 2 and the purple die is 5, then your base number is 11.*

4. Find the number you rolled on the green die on the left side of Table 2. Add the number in that row to your base number. *For example, if you rolled a 5, you would add 144 to your base number. The total of these numbers gives you your divinatory response. In the example above, the divinatory response would be 155 (11 + 144).*

Before reading your response you can check to make sure that the dice configuration shown at the top of the response corresponds to your roll. Please note that the first die shown is always blue, the second die purple, and the third die green. For example, the divinatory response chosen above (#155) will have this configuration.

Blue   Purple   Green

Finding Dice to Use

A special set of 3 dice (blue, purple and green) is available through Heartways Press. These dice have been specially blessed by the author for use in this process. Please see the order form at the back of this book if you wish to purchase these dice.

If you prefer, you can find your own dice and use them.

Try to get three different colors to make it easy and, if necessary, change the instructions to reflect the colors of your dice. Please do not use these dice for any other purpose and be sure to bless the dice before you use them.

If you cannot find different colored dice and want to begin using this book right away, use 1 die (any color) and roll it three times, consulting table 1 after the first and the second rolls and table 2 after the third roll.

The Divinatory
Responses

I

∎ ∎ ∎

YOU ARE THE WAY

You have heard me say, "I am the way, the truth and the life." That statement is equally true for you. The truth, the path to the divine, the life of the witness runs through your heart. There is no way, no truth, no life, except through you.

2

■ ■ ■

Your Essence

Your essence is unbroken, whole, dynamic and creative. It but awaits your trust.

3

The Jewel

You are one facet in the many-faceted jewel of God's love and grace. What makes one facet shine is available to all. The light that is in me is also in you.

4

THE FOUNTAIN

There is no one who will refuse love when it is offered without conditions. And who will offer it but you, my brother or sister? Today you will drink deeply from the fountain of my love. Tomorrow you will be the fountain.

5

MY FRIENDSHIP

You have available to you a personal relationship with
me. It comes into being as you begin to want it and trust
it. The simple but authentic need for my friendship is all
that is required.

6

UNHELPFUL THOUGHTS

Unhelpful thoughts must be witnessed lovingly and gently released. Then, only thoughts that bless and recall you to truth will remain.

7

HIDING THE TRUTH

You are a master at taking truth and inverting it. But just because you have inverted truth does not mean the truth ceases to be true. It means only that you have succeeded in hiding the truth from yourself.

8

Vigilance

Be vigilant. A single false idea can bring the mind that thinks it to despair. But a single true thought restores the kingdom.

9

AN OPEN DOOR

Truth is a door that remains open. You cannot close this door. You can choose not to enter. You can walk in the opposite direction. But you cannot say: "I tried to enter, but the door was closed." The door is never closed to you or anyone else.

IO

Not Seeking

It is not necessary to seek God, because God is already the essence of who you are. Simply remove all judgments and thoughts that do not bless you or others. Then the veil will be lifted.

II

SURRENDERING ILLUSIONS

As illusions are surrendered, truth appears. As separation is relinquished, the original unity emerges unchanged. When you stop pretending to be what you are not, what you are can be clearly seen.

12

THE FRIEND

The Friend is the one who has your greatest good at heart. The Friend is the one who also has the greatest good of others at heart. God and the Friend are always one. When you approach the Friend within, God hears your footsteps.

13

THE ORIGINAL SPARK

Within your heart and mind is the original spark of Creation. No matter where your life takes you, no matter how far you stray from the path, you cannot extinguish this spark within your consciousness. It was and is God's gift to you. When you acknowledge the spark and nurture it, the light within you grows until it completely surrounds you. Then, you too become the Friend, the Christ, the Buddha, the Compassionate One.

14

THE LIGHT OF TRUTH

The light of truth lives even in the darkest of places. There is no such thing as total absence of light. Darkness cannot exist except in reference to the light. All darkness is a journey toward light. No matter how great your pain, it is measured by the degree to which you feel love's absence or loss. All pain is a journey toward love without conditions.

15

THE LIGHT-BEARER

Once you find the light, no matter how insignificant it seems, your life will never be the same. A light-bearer never questions the light s/he carries. And so s/he can offer it to others patiently and without fear.

16

Overlooking Differences

Words and beliefs that separate you from others must be put aside. If you wish to walk in peace, find what you share with others and overlook the differences you see.

17

SEEING TRUTH

Truth comes in all shapes and sizes, but it remains one simple truth. You must learn to see the truth in every form and in each situation.

18

GOD HAS MANY WAYS

Do not think that those who follow a different path home will be denied salvation. God has many ways of bringing us home.

WORDS AND CONCEPTS

Words and concepts will not open your heart. Only love can open your heart.

20

THE QUALITIES OF LOVE

When you are connected to the love within your heart, the path opens before you. Actions flow spontaneously from you. There is no self-consciousness, ambivalence, or deliberation, for these are not the qualities of love.

21

SPIRITUALITY

To be spiritual is to see without judgment, to see not just with the eyes, but with the heart. When you look with the heart, you see beauty everywhere, even in suffering. Wherever hearts are touched by the poignancy of life, there is beauty. There is beauty in the rain and clouds, and beauty in the sunlight. There is beauty in aloneness and in intimacy, in laughter and in tears.

YOU ARE GOD'S CHILD

You are God's child, even as I am. All that is good and true about God is good and true about you. Accept this fact, even for an instant, and your life would be transformed. Accept this about your brother or sister, and all conflict between you would end.

23

A Simple Choice

You have a simple choice: to find each other innocent or to find each other guilty. This choice occurs over and over again, every day, every hour, every moment. Thought by thought, you imprison or release each other. And as you choose to treat others, so do you deliver the same judgment upon yourself.

24

The Mirror

Every judgment you make about your brother or sister states very specifically what you cannot accept about yourself. You never judge or dislike another person unless s/he reminds you of yourself.

25

ADMITTING YOUR MISTAKES

When you justify your mistakes, you hang onto them, forcing yourself to defend your actions over and over again. This takes a great deal of time and energy. Indeed, if you are not careful, it can become the dominant theme of your life.

Admit your mistakes and deliver yourself from pain, struggle, and deceit. There is no mistake that cannot be corrected. There is no trespass that cannot be forgiven.

26

NOT CONDEMNING

To condemn your sister for making mistakes is to pretend to be mistake free, which you are not. I asked you before and I will ask you again: which one of you will throw the first stone?

Instead of condemning your sister for her mistakes, release her from your judgment. To release her is to love her, for it places her where love alone lies, beyond judgment of any kind.

27

MAKING WRONG

To make wrong is to teach guilt and perpetuate the belief that punishment is necessary. To make right is to teach love and demonstrate forgiveness. To put it simply, you are never right to make wrong, or wrong to make right.

You cannot love in an unloving way. You can't be right and attack what's wrong.

28

FREEDOM FROM GUILT

No matter what you have said or done, you do not deserve to suffer. Your suffering will not feed the hungry or heal the sick.

Forgive yourself and come back into your life with a clear vision and a strong heart. Your freedom from guilt serves not just you, but also those who need your kind deeds and your compassionate understanding.

29

No Exceptions

Not one of God's children can be evil. At worst he is hurt. At worst he attacks others and blames them for his pain. But he is not evil.

Yes, your compassion must go this deep. There is no human being that does not deserve your forgiveness. There is no human being that does not deserve your love.

30

THE LAW OF EQUALITY

Your good and that of your brother or sister are one and the same. You cannot advance your life by hurting another, nor can you help another by hurting yourself. All attempts to break this simple equation lead to suffering and despair.

3I

No Sacrifice

Make others equally important. Do not sacrifice for them or ask them to sacrifice for you, but help them when you can and receive their help gratefully when you need it.

More than this is too much. Less than this is too little.

32

FORGIVING YOURSELF

You have only one person to forgive in your journey and that is yourself. You are the judge. You are the jury. And you are the prisoner.

33

INTERPRETATION

How you interpret your experience is rather important. Are you receiving your experience as a blessing or as a punishment? That is the question you must ask yourself.

Everything in your experience can be endowed with spiritual qualities by bringing your love, acceptance or forgiveness to it.

34

PURPOSE OF EXPERIENCE

All experience happens for one purpose only: to expand your awareness. Any other meaning you see in your life is a meaning that you made up.

When you see the world in its utter neutrality, you will understand that it exists only as a tool for your learning.

35

YOUR BROTHER'S KEEPER

Whenever you take another person into your heart, you open the door to me as well. There is no person who is not dear to me. I see into the soul of both the criminal and his victim. I see both calling for love and acceptance, and I will not refuse them. Do not be shocked that I ask the same of you, who are my hands, my feet, and my voice in the world.

36

⸬ ⸬ •

Taking Advantage

To honor and care for yourself is your responsibility. Anything that honors you cannot possibly hurt another. But to act in a selfish way, placing your good above that of another, invites conflict and resentment.

The ways of the world are harsh in this regard. One who takes advantage of others may be feared but he is not loved. When his fortune changes, which it invariably does, others are more than happy to help pull him down.

37

WITHHOLDING LOVE

Only by recognizing the worthiness of others is your own worthiness confirmed. When you withhold your love, your enemy is not the only one who is denied that blessing. You are denied it too.

38

UNSELFISH GIVING

When you give without thought of return, the law of grace manifests through you. True giving is an overflowing of your love. You don't feel that you are being depleted when you give in this way. In fact, you feel energized, because the love you give returns to you through the gratitude of others whom you have touched.

39

LOVING YOUR ENEMY

Your enemy sees your weaknesses and does his or her best to exploit them. If you have a blind spot, you can be sure your enemy sees it. S/he shows you exactly where your fears and insecurities lie. Only one who opposes you thus can be such an effective teacher.

When you learn to love your enemy, you demonstrate your willingness to look at all of the dark places within your mind. Your enemy is the mirror into which you look until the angry face that you see smiles back at you.

40

RESOLVING CONFLICT

Peace comes when love and mutual respect are present. Conflict is caused when people dehumanize each other or see each other as unworthy. In this case, even the simplest details cannot be negotiated. But let each person bring to the other an attitude of respect and acceptance, and even difficult details can be resolved.

41

STANDING UP FOR YOURSELF

While I encourage you to take issue with actions that are uncaring, hurtful, or disrespectful to you or others, I ask you to do so in a loving way. Do so in a way that respects the people whose actions you oppose. For they are your brothers and sisters too.

42

SAYING NO WITH LOVE

You can say "no" to other people's demands without casting them out of your heart. You may not be able to give them what they want, but you can find a way to support them that affirms both of you.

This is how the lover treats the beloved. S/he accepts their equality. S/he knows that the needs of one cannot be more important than the needs of the other. Both people need to be honored and respected.

43

LOVING THE VICTIMIZER

It is not the man who strikes out at you, but the boy who is feeling overwhelmed, scared, and rejected. Do not let your sight be distorted by the angry, disdainful face of the man. Beneath that hard exterior is overwhelming pain and self judgment. Beneath the mask of mismanaged manhood and vicious anger is the boy who does not believe he is lovable.

If you cannot embrace the boy in him, how can you embrace the boy or the girl in yourself? For his fear and yours are not so different.

44

BRINGING LOVE

To oppose or argue with a false idea is to strengthen it. That is the way of violence. My way is nonviolent. It demonstrates the answer in its approach to the problem. It brings love, not attack, to the ones in pain. Its means are consistent with its ends.

45

CRUCIFIXION

Crucifixion happens when your heart closes to your brother. Resurrection happens when you open your heart to him, when you learn to love him as you love yourself.

46

The Freedom of Others

When you love without conditions, you support the freedom of others to choose their own way, even when you disagree with them. You trust them to make the best choice for them. You know that they can never make a mistake that will cut them off from God's love or from yours.

47

THE POWER OF ACCEPTANCE

Love says: "I accept you as you are. I consider your good equally with my own." Do you have any idea how powerful this statement is? To every person you address in this way, you offer freedom from suffering. And by offering it to him, you offer it to yourself.

48

ENTERING INTO PARTNERSHIP

Your decision to enter into partnership should not be based on a desire to avoid looking at yourself, but on a willingness to intensify that process. Relationship is like a giant backhoe. It digs down through the superficial layers of consciousness and exposes your deepest fears and insecurities. If you aren't willing to look this deeply, you might want to question your desire to be in an intimate relationship. You can't get close to another person without coming face to face with yourself.

49

SELF BETRAYAL

The emotional high of a new relationship promises more than it can deliver. If you experience "falling in love," you can be sure that you will experience "falling out of love." The very expression "falling in love'" should tell you that this experience is about self-betrayal.

50

YOUR LIFE PARTNER

Your life partner usually doesn't look like you expect him or her to look. S/he doesn't arrive with smoke and mirrors. S/he doesn't come in a perfect shape or size. If you look only at the exterior, you won't recognize this person. You must look beneath the surface.

Your life partner is genuine and authentic with you. S/he is not the one who dazzles you with big promises and expensive gifts, but the one who readily takes your hand and looks into your eyes without fear.

THE FEAR OF INTIMACY

Some people are afraid of love. When you are aloof,
they feel safe and desire your presence. But when you come
close, they get scared and ask you to back off or go away.
This emotionally teasing behavior enables them to be in
relationship while avoiding intimacy and commitment. If
you are drawn into such a relationship, you must face the
fact that you too may be afraid to receive love. Why else
would you choose a partner who is afraid to give it?

52

Marriage

Marriage is not a promise to be together throughout all eternity, for no one can promise that. It is a promise to be present "now." It is a vow that must be renewed in each moment if it is to have meaning.

53

TENDING YOUR GARDEN

Don't allow your happiness to be dependent on your partner's happiness. That will just drag both of you down. Tend to your own garden, and offer your partner a rose to smell. Refusing to tend your garden and complaining that your partner never gives you roses will not make either one of you feel better.

54

VALIDATION

When you and your partner have difficulty validating each other, your relationship goes into crisis. You need to catch this downward spiral before it goes out of control. Take some time to center yourself and get in touch with what the relationship means to you. Come back into your heart. Find a way to validate your partner and ask him or her respectfully for the validation you need.

55

⚃ ⚀ ⚀

"WE" CONSCIOUSNESS

When love is present in a relationship, the question is always "What are *we* going to do?" not "What am *I* going to do?" You want what is best for your relationship. Finding that shared reality helps you and your partner grow beyond narrow self-interest and begin to serve the higher purpose of your union.

56

FORGIVING EACH OTHER

Forgiveness is the key to success in every relationship. Through the practice of forgiveness, imperfect people become whole, and broken relationships are healed and strengthened. You learn what real love and real essence are all about.

57

⚃ ⚁ ⚁

PARENTAL WOUNDS

When you come to peace with your parents and accept them as equals, you no longer wish to change to meet their expectations, nor do you want them to change to meet yours. Moreover, you stop creating parental lessons in your intimate relationships. If you are a man, you stop finding your mother in your wife and trying to be her husband. If you are a woman, you stop finding your father in your husband and trying to be his wife.

58

⚃ ⚃ ⚂

FATHER AND MOTHER

Father's love teaches courage; mother's love teaches gentleness. With courage, you walk through your fears. With gentleness, you open your heart.

Problems with the father translate as an inability to understand and fulfill your creative life purpose. Problems with the mother translate as an inability to develop loving, intimate, relationships.

59

⚃ ⚄ ⚁

THE SOUL MATE

The soul-mate cannot manifest until there is honesty and clarity in all of your relationships. You cannot find the soul-mate by abandoning any other human being. You must be right with all of your relationships.

60

SEEKING THE BELOVED

If your life is anchored in the truth of your experience, then that truth can be shared. But if you are looking for truth, or love, or salvation outside yourself, you will be disappointed again and again.

Only by honoring yourself does the beloved come. Those who twist themselves into pretzels in the search for love simply push the beloved away.

61

Love is Beyond Form

Relationships constantly change form. Children grow up and become parents; parents surrender their bodies to the next adventure; friends move apart; lovers break up. Growth continues.

Forms come and go. That is the bittersweet quality of life. If you become attached to the form or throw away the love just because the form is changing, you will suffer unnecessarily.

Let the form go when it is time and your love for this person can continue unimpeded. Conditional love can be transformed into love without conditions.

62

ENDING AN AGREEMENT

Not all relationships are meant to last a lifetime. Some are temporary learning experiences lasting a few months or a few years. Shame about making a mistake in partnership does not serve anyone.

When one person no longer wants to keep an agreement, the agreement is off. You can't hold another person against his or her will. If you try to do so, you will push love away.

Love survives the ending of agreements, if you will allow it to. If you won't, you only cheat yourself.

63

SEPARATION

It is not easy when a relationship ends or changes form, and gentleness on both sides is extremely important if healing is to happen for both people.

Be grateful for what you have learned with your partner. Be cognizant of the issues that separated you and take responsibility for your part in them.

Don't blame yourself or the other person. Neither one of you is bad or wrong. Instead, accept the situation exactly as it is. Send love to your partner and yourself.

Healing takes time and loving intentions. Be patient, compassionate, and forgiving. Don't get in the way of healing by holding grievances or resentments.

64

THE FREEDOM TO LOVE

Love and freedom are inseparable. You cannot love if you do not have a choice. The great tragedy is not that you and your partner may decide to part. That is sad perhaps, but not tragic. The real tragedy is that you and your partner may decide to stay together or separate because you believe that you have no other choice. If there is love, there must be the freedom to choose.

65

CONTROL

Your experience of love will be diminished in direct proportion to your need to control it. Control places conditions upon that which must be without conditions. When you establish conditions on love, you experience the conditions, not the love. You encounter the form, not the content.

66

REVELATION

Sit for a moment in profound forgiveness of yourself and other people. Stop reacting. Stop withholding your love or pushing the love of others away.

Just be present. Be with your experience without defending it. Accept the experience of others without judging it or trying to change it. As you sit in the stillness, feel how it blesses you. Feel how your pain and struggle dissolve as you cease judging and interpreting your life or the lives of others.

This is how revelation begins. When you let go of judgment, peace comes. When you stop finding fault with your life, the love energy of the universe rises to support you.

67

DETACHMENT

True detachment comes from familiarity with others, not from estrangement. Distancing others does not bring detachment. Only when you let others into your heart do you become capable of releasing them.

68

ONE LOVE FOR ALL

When you have learned to consider one person's good equally with your own, you become capable of doing it with others. Then, no one is excluded from your love.

Real Love is the end of separate thoughts, separate agendas, separate wills. It has one thought, one agenda, one will, one love for all beings.

69

LIFE IS A WORK OF ART

Your life is a work of art and you need to be busy about it even as a bee is busy pollinating flowers. And remember, work that is not joyful to you accomplishes nothing of value in the world.

PREFERENCES

You cannot say that what one person builds with his life is less valuable than what another person builds. All you can say in truth is that you prefer what one person has built to what another has built. You have your preferences.

Fortunately, God does not share them. Not yours or anyone else's. God listens to everyone's story. Her ear is to each person's heart.

71

Embracing the Gift

Whatever gift you have to give is the perfect one. It does not matter if it is not the one you thought you would have or the one you wanted. When you embrace the gift, the purpose of your life reveals itself. You see how every lesson, every problem, every moment of suffering was absolutely necessary for the gift to be given and received.

Unquestionable Gifts

God does not give questionable gifts. Often, you will not know the meaning of the gift until it is put to work in your life.

The gifts of God do not feed your ego expectations. They help you open to your true nature and purpose here. Sometimes they seem to close a door and you don't understand why. Only when the right door opens do you realize why the wrong door was closed.

73

WHAT YOU VALUE

What you deeply value has your full, loving attention. It is nurtured, watered, and brought into fullness. It does not happen overnight. It does not happen exactly how or when you want it to. It flourishes through your commitment, your constancy, your devotion.

What you love prospers. It unfolds. It gets roots and wings.

74

WITHHOLDING YOUR GIFTS

The gifts you have been given in this life do not belong to you alone. They belong to everyone. Do not be selfish and withhold them.

Consider how empty life would be if others around you chose to abandon their gifts. All that you find wonderful in life—the music, the poetry, the films, the sports, the laughter—would vanish if others withheld their gifts from you.

Do not withhold your gift from others. Do not make the mistake of thinking that you have no gift to give.

75

THE SEARCH FOR APPROVAL

The search for approval stems from a lack of valuing of self. When you don't value yourself, you seek validation from others. Unfortunately, others are not always able to give you the approval or recognition that you seek.

When you look to others to validate you so that you can have faith and confidence in yourself, you are putting the cart before the horse. Learn to love and value yourself first. Then appreciation will naturally flow your way.

NURTURING YOUR GIFT

No matter how anxious you are to grow up with your gift, you must first take the time to nurture and develop it. Find a good teacher. Sing for your friends and family members. Take small risks, then bigger ones. Gradually, you will gain skill and confidence. Then, without doing anything, the audiences will grow.

Happy people express their gifts on whatever level and in whatever arena life offers them. Unhappy people hold onto their gifts until life gives them the perfect venue.

AUTHENTICITY

If you are true to yourself, you will neither conform to the expectations of others nor will you isolate yourself from their feedback.

The desire for approval prevents honest self-expression. It is soft and apologetic. The need to shock or offend others prevents dialogue and intimacy. It pushes people away.

Authentic expression is neither offensive nor apologetic. It tells its truth and invites dialogue. It builds bridges of understanding between people.

78

THE RADIANT SELF

When faced with your uncompromising commitment to yourself, others either join you or move swiftly out of your way. Grey spaces created by your ambivalence—your desire to have something and give it up at the same time—move toward yea or nay, undoing co-dependency, neurotic bargaining for love, apathy and critical behavior.

Your willingness to live your dream explodes the entire edifice of fear that surrounds you. It is that simple. And it all happens as gently as the first "yes" said in the silence of your heart.

79

THE WORK OF SPIRIT

If your work is not joyful, if it doesn't express your unique talents and abilities, and if it doesn't uplift others, then it is not spiritual work. Spiritual work is done joyfully. It brings happiness to you and to others. The means are consistent with the ends. The process and the goal are united.

80

SACRIFICE OR GREED

Do not cheat yourself by working out of sacrifice. Do not cheat others by working out of greed.

Do not deny yourself what you need to live with dignity. Do not take more than you need.

Poverty will not bring you salvation. Material wealth will not bring you happiness.

81

SURRENDER

Having found your lifework, the greatest obstacle to its fulfillment lies in your attempt to "direct" it. You cannot make your spiritual work happen. If you try, you will fail.

Spiritual work requires surrender. Worldly work requires the illusion of control.

As soon as you give up the need to control, any work can become spiritual. As soon as you try to take charge, the most spiritual projects begin to fall apart.

Spiritual Rewards

God does not necessarily reward spiritual work with material success. All rewards are spiritual. Happiness, joy, compassion, peace, sensitivity: these are the rewards for a life lived in integrity.

You must learn, once and for all, to stop measuring spiritual riches with a worldly yardstick. Don't make the mistake of thinking that your lifework must bring in a large paycheck. On the other hand, don't make the mistake of thinking that you must be poor to serve God.

It matters not how much you hold in your hands, but whether your hands are extended outward to your brother or sister.

83

COMMITMENT

Having a goal means nothing if you are not committed to it. If you are not willing to devote your time, energy and attention toward achieving your goal, then your dreams may not manifest outwardly.

When you get really honest with yourself, you know that no one else is preventing you from realizing your goals. You are the only person who can sabotage your dreams.

84

UNCONFLICTED DESIRE

If you say "no" to what you don't want, and "yes" to what you do want, it won't be difficult for you to create the life you desire. It becomes complicated only when you don't know what you want or when you don't trust your heart's desire.

Take time to find out what you want. When there is unconflicted desire in your heart, your creative process flows easily.

85

CO-CREATION

All creation is really co-creation. You determine what you want, commit to it, move toward it, and the opportunities you need to realize your goal come your way. To be sure, you must keep surrendering your expectations. You must be open to the opportunities that arise, but you do not have to make them happen.

One of the great "Ahahs" on the spiritual path is the recognition that you don't have to make your life happen. It happens by itself.

The Truth Within

You cannot experience joy in life by following the dreams and agendas of other people. You experience joy only by remaining faithful to the truth within your heart.

87

SEE THE LIGHT IN OTHERS

Do not focus on the darkness in others, for it is not ultimately real. Focus, instead, on the indwelling goodness of all beings.

Do not focus on what is missing or what needs to be corrected. Focus on what is always there and can never be taken away.

Because you do not look for weaknesses, you will help people find their strength. Because you do not look for wounds, you will help people find their gratitude.

HEALING YOURSELF

Your job is not to heal other people, but to heal your-self. Your healing belongs not just to you, but to everyone.

Being a healer means accepting your inherent capacity to be free of conflict, free of guilt, free of judgment or blame. Accept this capacity in yourself and you will demonstrate miracles in your life just as I did.

89

THE MINISTRY OF LOVE

When you learn to love yourself, you cannot help loving others. It happens spontaneously.

There is no limit on the love that you can give or receive. It constantly recycles, flowing in and out of the heart. Like waves breaking and receding on a beach, the tides of love are steady and dependable. They touch every shoreline with their blessing.

Love is not something you do. Love is who you are. You are the embodiment of love in this moment. Nothing less.

LOVE'S PATIENT BLESSING

When I heard the call, I answered it. Now you hear it too and wherever you go, love goes with you. Love moves with your legs, reaches with your hands, speaks with your voice, and sees with your eyes.

The challenge before you is a simple one: "Whatever is not loving must be forgiven." Forgiveness is love's patient blessing on an imperfect world.

You are the Door

As soon as you make space for God in your heart, S/He brings the stranger to your doorstep. As soon as you make space for God in your community, S/He brings the outcasts and the disenfranchised into the sanctuary of your church.

That is the way of Spirit. When you offer love, those who are in need of that love will find you. They are brought to God through your loving presence.

THE ONLY QUESTION

There is only one question I can ask you: "Are you happy right now?"

If the answer is "yes," then you are already in heaven. If the answer is "no," then I ask "why not?"

You may give me thirty pages of testimony as to why you are unhappy, but I will simply ask again "why not?" And sooner or later, you will realize that all your reasons for not being happy are about the past.

All I can do is ask "Why not now?" I am not interested in your past or future.

93

THE SEED OF FAITH

Dig deeply in the garden of your faith and you will find the voices of truth that will help you open your heart to love's presence. Regardless of the tradition you belong to, you must find the seed, separate it from the husk, and see that it is planted in your lifetime.

You must find the core teaching that connects you to love and pass that teaching on to your children. That is the only way that a tradition stays healthy.

A barren tree will make no fruit. A religion that does not help its followers connect to love will not prosper.

CULTS

Cults thrive on the insecurity of their members. In the name of spiritual surrender, initiates are asked to capitulate to the authority structure of the cult.

Hierarchical, closed belief systems promise Shangri-La and deliver Alcatraz. They promise freedom from suffering and deliver physical abuse and mind control.

You can't prevent people from being drawn into such situations, but you can offer them a helping hand when they are ready to get out.

95

LOVE, NOT AGREEMENT

Tolerance for differences is essential to the creation of a safe, loving space. It is not necessary for people to have the same beliefs to experience spiritual communion with one another. Communion happens through the extension of love and non-judgment. It can happen anywhere, with any group of people, if they are committed to loving and respecting one another. Love, not agreement, must become the bond that holds the community together.

96

TOLERANCE OF DIFFERENCES

A society that tolerates differences in ideas and perspectives is a society that is based on the practical demonstration of love and equality. Equality between people requires that all ideas be heard and all perspectives be considered. The path to truth has never been an easy one. It certainly has never been one based on expediency.

97

A HEALING COMMUNITY

A living church is a therapeutic, healing community, but without any therapists or healers. It invites you get out of the way and trust Spirit to heal. When you try to become the healer, the minister, the teacher, you just add more confusion, fear and guilt to everybody's plate.

A living church does not offer techniques for fixing or salvation. It provides a safe space and invites you to share your experience with others. It asks you to help create that safe space by being a gentle witness to others. That is all. That is enough for a lifetime.

OPEN MIND/OPEN HEART

You cannot foster an open mind if you teach any dogma. Giving people answers is manipulative and controlling. Instead, help people articulate their questions and begin the search for their own answers.

You cannot foster open-heartedness if you exclude anyone from your community or give preferential treatment to any member. People open their hearts when they feel welcome and treated as equals. Nothing closes the heart down quicker than competition for love and attention.

99

⚃ ⚁ ⚂

SANCTUARY

Through the practice of voluntary confession, a community of equals is born. No one is more spiritual than anyone else. Each person has his or her own fears and judgments and wishes to release them.

Sacred space is created when the members of the community hold their ego material compassionately. Then, each movement of fear can be gently acknowledged and released. Then, the heart and mind close only to open more fully to the presence of love.

REAL LOVE

Real love is unconditional. It does not exclude anyone for any reason. It requires you to see beyond appearances, to see others from an inner conviction that all people carry the divine spark within them.

Real love does not seek to bind, control, or enslave, but to liberate, to empower, to set others free to find their own truth.

Some people like to play at surrender. They talk about love, but keep a hard shell around them which pushes love away. They have the semblance of love, but not the real thing. Real love would crack their lives open.

101

SCARCITY THINKING

Scarcity thinking results from your perception that you are not worthy of love. When you do not feel worthy of love, you project lack outside you.

The experience of scarcity is not God punishing you. It is you showing yourself a belief that needs to be corrected.

Abundance comes into your life, not because you have learned to memorize some mumbo jumbo incantation, but because you have learned to bring love to the wounded aspects of your psyche. Love heals all perception of lack and division, restoring the original perception of wholeness, free of shame or guilt.

102

ABUNDANCE

Contrary to popular opinion, abundance does not mean that you have a lot of money or material possessions. Abundance means that you have what you need, use it wisely, and give what you don't need to others. Your life has poise, balance, and integrity. You don't have too little. You don't have too much.

The abundant person has no more or less than she can use responsibly and productively. She does not obsess on protecting what she has or in obtaining what she does not need. She is content with what she has, and is open to giving and receiving all the resources that God brings into her life.

THE LAW OF ENERGY

If you are loving, you receive love, because love always returns to itself. If you demand love, you receive demands for love.

As you sow, so do you reap. The law of energy is circular. What goes out comes back and what comes back goes out. You receive what you give and you give what you receive.

When you know this, the whole chess game falls apart. The mystery is revealed.

THE EGO'S AGENDA

Your ego's agenda operates from the belief that you can manipulate people and events to obtain the outcome you want. This agenda is selfish and short-sighted. It does not consider the good of others, and therefore it does not consider your ultimate good.

When you cheat someone out of something s/he deserves, you lose not only what you thought you would gain; you also lose what you would have gained if you had acted in a less selfish way. Every attempt to gain in a selfish manner eventually leads to loss and defeat, because selfish actions are not supported by the universal energy.

105

GRACE VS. STRUGGLE

Grace happens when you abide with what is. Struggle happens when you push what is away or try to bring something else in. Grace happens when you accept. Struggle happens when you reject.

Grace is not continuous for anyone. No matter how far the heart has opened, there will be times when it still contracts in fear. That is to be expected. Grace comes and goes. Alignment happens and is lost.

All this is part of the great dance. Since the dance never happens the way you expect it to, you have to be ready to dance with whatever comes. If struggle happens and you dance with it, grace eventually returns.

106

MOVE WITH THE WIND

When conditions are right for something to happen, it will happen without great effort. When conditions are not right, even great effort will not succeed.

Like a tree dancing in a storm, you need to move with the wind, not against it. Know your needs, but allow them to be met as life knows how. Do not insist that your needs be met in a certain way. The trunk of the tree snaps when it tries to stand against the wind.

Don't force your life. Don't try to make things happen before their time.

107

RECOGNIZING ESSENCE

When you feel unloved, unworthy or cut off from others, you are forgetting the Essence within you, which is wholly lovable and loving. When you are in touch with your Essence, you know that you are acceptable exactly as you are. There is nothing about you (or anyone else) that needs to be improved or fixed. To know your Essence, you must discard your self-judgments, as well as your criticisms of others.

108

BUDDHA'S WINDOW

Don't choose one side of the argument. Learn to take both sides and work toward the middle. Both extremes reflect each other. Those who are in conflict share the same lesson.

There is only one way to freedom. Buddha called it *The Middle Way,* the way between extremes. You can't get there by taking sides.

When you can observe the argument without taking sides, when you can be in the middle of the battle without attacking anyone, then you have arrived in the place where the lotus blooms. You have slipped through the veil. You are no longer an object blocking the light, but the window that allows the light to stream through.

109

LIFTING THE VEIL

God is within. God isn't in how life appears. That's just the veil. To see the truth, you must lift the veil.

If you aren't looking for God within your own heart, you can live your whole life and never know that God exists. You can be bitter, resentful, or angry.

An about-face is necessary. You must turn to the place where God abides. You must find the place in you that is unconditionally aligned with love.

You can't do this while you are blaming others or holding onto grievances. Nor can you do it when you are feeling guilty and beating yourself up for making mistakes. All judgment of self and other must go. You must come to God with open arms.

110

⬛ ⬛ ⬛

RELATIONSHIP WITH GOD

God's presence in your life is totally unique. Don't accept concepts of God that come from others or make the mistake of thinking that someone else has more spiritual knowledge than you do. Cultivate your relationship with God directly. Enter the silence of your own heart. Pray and ask for guidance. Open the dialogue and listen for God''s answers within and in the signs that She sends into your life. And know absolutely that any message of fear does not come from God or from any of Her ministers.

III

THE HIGHEST TRUTH

You come to oneness not through conformity, but through authenticity. When you have the courage to be yourself, you find the highest truth you are capable of receiving. Finding the highest truth in yourself, you recognize that truth when you see it manifest in others.

112

Not Prescribing

Freedom comes when you reject all forms of external authority and when you refuse to be an authority for anyone else. Paradoxically, that is also the moment in which the self becomes Self.

113

THE BELIEFS YOU ACCEPT

Ultimately, you alone are responsible for the beliefs you accept. Someone can tell you terrible lies, but it won't be his responsibility that you believed them. So don't waste your time blaming the authority figures you listened to.

Everybody at one time or another gives his power away, only to learn to take it back. That is an important and profound lesson on the spiritual path. Be grateful if you have learned this lesson. It means you are closer to your own truth, and if you are closer to your own truth, you are closer to God, the Universal Truth.

114

THE AUTHORITY OF THE HEART

True authority is rock-solid and self-nurtured. It moves toward its greatest joy without harming others.

The true authority of your heart does not need to please others at its expense, nor does it need to please itself at the expense of others. It is content to be what it is and to allow others to be what they are.

115

FACING YOUR FEARS

Before you can become the light-bearer, you must walk through your own darkness. The bearer of the light does not deny the darkness, but walks through it.

When there is nothing about yourself or anyone else that you are afraid to look at, the darkness has no more hold over you. Then you can walk through the darkness and be the light.

Where does light come from? It comes from you. Once you stop playing the victim and face your fears, the atmosphere that surrounds you brightens. In your blessing of yourself, the entire world is forgiven.

116

HEAVEN ON EARTH

When does the kingdom of Heaven come to Earth? As soon as you are willing to open your heart and walk through your fears. When does the Messiah come? No, not later, but now.

Do not place salvation in the future or it will never come. Ask for it now. Accept it now. God's kingdom manifests in this moment only.

When does Heaven come? When this moment is enough. When this place is enough. When this friend is enough. When these events and circumstances are acceptable. When you no longer crave something other than what stands before you.

MIRACLES

Miracles come spontaneously to the heart that has opened and to the mind that has surrendered its need to control or to know.

118

GOD'S PLAN

God doesn't ask you to chop off your intellect and believe on faith. S/He makes a far more simple request: "Just stop judging, stop finding fault, stop trying to make life conform to your pictures of reality."

When you experience your life free of the limitations you would place upon it, problems resolve. Relationships move on course. You stop interfering with God's plan.

What is God's plan? It is healing, reconciliation, joyful self-expression and intimate communion. God's agenda is to allow the miraculous to happen at all times.

119

MIRACLE-MINDEDNESS

Visualization can be powerful. It can alter perception and assist in healing. But I wouldn't suggest that you tie yourself to the train tracks and visualize the train disappearing as it approaches you at sixty miles per hour.

Miracles are not demonstrated through the attempt to manipulate physical reality. That is an activity of the ego.

Miracles are demonstrated when you surrender to your experience and connect with God's will for you in each moment. Your job is not to try to alter physical reality but to be fully present with it.

The Door is not Important

When you are a loving presence, people will come home to the true Self through you. You see, it does not matter who the door is. It could be me. It could be you. It could be another brother or sister. The door does not need to be celebrated.

When the door needs to be celebrated, it ceases to be a door. When people grasp the finger pointing to the moon, they can no longer tell where it is pointing.

121

RELEASING THE OUTCOME

One who loves without conditions is never attached to the outcome. People come and go and you never know the whys and wherefores. You think that some people will easily pass through the gate, yet they turn suddenly away. You are convinced that others will never come within sight of the gate, yet they cross the threshold with unexpected grace.

Do not be concerned. It is none of your business who comes and who goes. The covenant is made in every heart and only God knows who is ready and who is not.

THE STEADY FLAME

Don't look outside of yourself for answers. Don't seek refuge in the ideas and opinions of other people. Surrender all of that, and seek the place where love begins, in your own heart.

When the spark in your heart is attended to, it grows into a steady flame. When the flame is fed by acts of loving kindness to self and others, it becomes a blazing fire, a source of warmth and light for all who encounter it.

123

REMEMBERING GOD

I do not ask you to meditate or pray for an hour a day, although there is nothing wrong with this. I simply ask you to remember God for five minutes out of each hour, or for one thought out of every ten. Nine thoughts may be about needing to fix yourself or someone else, but let the tenth thought be about that which does not need fixing. Let the tenth thought be about something which is totally acceptable, totally lovable.

124

THE SILENCE OF THE HEART

All the answers that you need can be found in the silence of your heart. You don't have to look to others for solutions or advice. You don't need to practice elaborate systems of meditation or yoga. Simply cease judging, interpreting, and speculating. Let all that is not "being" fall away and "being" will flower of itself.

125

A Helpful Practice

Whenever you are confused, anxious, fearful, or angry, ask yourself "Am I loving myself right now?" This question reminds you that beneath all fearful thoughts and behaviors lies the refusal to be gentle and loving toward yourself.

Even if your anger or upset feelings are directed toward someone else, you aren't being loving toward yourself. Indeed, the only way that you can be angry at anyone else is to forget to love yourself.

Your only responsibility while here in this embodiment is to love and take care of yourself. When love is established in your heart, it flows automatically to others.

126

NOT READY TO BLESS

A practice that will help you stay centered is to refrain from speaking or acting when you are not ready to bless others. By refusing to make others guilty, you interrupt the cycle of blame and shame. You don't engage their pain with your pain, their anger with your anger, or their unworthiness with your own.

Because you speak and act only when you are able to bless, you stand free of the painful drama of mutual trespass and betrayal. You take care of yourself and others at the deepest level of being. Waves of illusion wash over you, but you stand simply and firmly in the truth that you are.

127

ILLUSIONS

Illusions are born when you stop loving another person or yourself. The only way to dissolve illusions is to start loving right now in this moment.

128

A Tiny Light

God's love cannot be abused. It can be rejected, denied, hidden. But all rejection, denial, and secret guilt have limits. Truth can be distorted but it can never be completely eradicated or denied. A tiny light always remains in the deepest darkness. And that light will always be found when the desire to find it arises.

129

FALLING FROM GRACE

People who do "evil" acts feel separate from God and from others. They feel unloved and act in unloving ways. But God has not stopped loving them. God is not able to stop loving anyone. For God is love, always love, in every moment.

Sin is but a temporary moment of separation. It cannot be final. Every child who falls from grace will return, because it is too painful to be separate from the Source of love. When the pain becomes too great, every wounded child turns back. There are no exceptions.

130

An Unforgiving Place

Peace will not come to the world until it comes into your heart. And it cannot come into your heart as long as you see enemies or "evil" people outside of you. Every evil you perceive in the world points to an unforgiving place in your heart that is calling out for healing.

131

⚅ ⚄ ⚅

SEE NO EVIL

Evil does not exist apart from your judgments. Every devil you see comes from the projection of your shame.

Do not see the drama happening outside of you or you will lose the key to the kingdom. The drama of shame and blame is happening only in your mind and that is where it must be dealt with.

You are the one who holds the key to the kingdom. If you offer committed love, nothing less can be returned to you.

132

FROM WOUNDS TO WINGS

If you keep looking for the devil in others, you will not find him. The devil is your own angelic presence defiled. It is all of your forgetting, all of your self-violation.

This recalcitrant being lives inside of you. He is the scared, unhappy child who feels unfairly treated and manipulates others in his search for acceptance. He is formidable only because you refuse to love him. Don't reject him anymore. Take him in your arms and hold him. Speak gently to him. When you have embraced the child within, his angelic presence is revealed. In your love, his fall is broken, and his wounds begin to heal.

133

DARK NIGHT OF THE SOUL

You cannot come to God if you don't go through the dark night of the soul. Your fear and your shame must be raised. Your feelings of separation must come up for healing. How can you rise from the ashes of your pain unless you acknowledge the pain?

If you pretend the wound isn't there, you can't begin your spiritual journey. Don't deny that it hurts, brother and sister. Come into your pain. It is not what you think it is.

When you have the courage to approach the wall of your fear, it turns into a doorway. Come through this door. I am waiting for you on the other side.

134

⚃ ⚀ ⚃

ACCEPTING GOD

When you accept God back into your life, your whole experience of the world and all the people in it changes. You are a father and a mother to every child who approaches you, a son or daughter to every elderly person. You are a friend to friend and friendless alike. And you are a lover to the one who remembers s/he is loved and to the one who has forgotten.

135

PAIN IS A MESSENGER

Pain is a messenger. It brings awareness. It tells you where and how you have betrayed yourself. That is important. Until you are aware of the self-violation, your journey to healing cannot begin.

Pain is not a punishment. It is a call to become conscious, to raise your hidden suffering into awareness.

⊡ ⊡ ⊡

INVITING TRESPASS

Every abusive relationship offers you the opportunity to say no to what does not honor you. Saying "no" to another person, of course, implies an awareness that you have tended to say "yes" in the past.

You establish the conditions for abuse by accepting conditional love. You say "yes" to self-degradation in exchange for the security you want. You say "yes" to fear by bargaining for love.

Now you know it will not work. Love cannot be bargained for. You cannot receive from others what you are unable or unwilling to give to yourself.

⚃ ⚃ ⚄

Moving Through Pain

Even your pain can be a doorway. It can make you aware of energies that are blocked in your body and in your life.

Don't deny your pain. Acknowledge it and move through it. Healing means movement. It doesn't mean falling in love with pain or building an identity around it.

Pain is universal. It touches every life at one time or another. But it does not have to be a constant companion. It is just a messenger.

To say that the messenger is not present when he is standing at your door is utter foolishness. You need to answer the door and hear what he has to say. But when the message has been heard, the messenger can leave. His job is over.

138

⁙ ⁙ ⁙

A True Healer

If you are a true healer, you respect the inner healing ability of your clients. You help your clients make the connections they are ready to make. You advocate integration, gentleness, and patience. As a result, your clients get stronger. They heal and move on.

As a true healer, you encourage your clients to avoid the extremes of denying their pain or embellishing it. Pain must be faced, not imagined. If it is there, it will express itself authentically. It will speak with its own voice in its own time. You must be careful not to put words in your clients' mouths or to pressure them to speak before they are ready.

139

HEALING TRAUMA

Finding out what happened to you is the first step in the process of healing trauma. Secrets need to be disclosed or discovered.

Don't deny what happened. Don't make it up. Just acknowledge what happened and be with it. That is what initiates the shift from untruth to truth, from secrets to revelation, from hidden discomfort to the conscious awareness of pain.

140

The Dream of Abuse

The Self is unassailable. You cannot put holes in it. You cannot pretend to hurt or be hurt. You cannot be separated from the Source of love, because you are love incarnate. You are the shining one dreaming the dream of abuse.

Pretending to be an angel when you feel like an abused kid does not contribute to your awakening. But neither does holding onto the wound.

When the wound is addressed with love, it heals. The healing can be instantaneous or it can take a lifetime, but victimization does stop and healing does happen. The drama of suffering does comes to an end.

141

RE-PARENTING YOURSELF

From the time you were an infant, you were conditioned to value yourself only when people responded positively to you. By contrast, in the process of healing, you learn to value yourself as you are, here and now, without conditions. Thus, you are "born again," or "re-parented," not by other authority figures, but by the Source of Love inside yourself.

No one else can do this for you. People can assist and encourage, but no one can teach you how to love yourself unconditionally. That is the work of each individual soul.

142

⚃ ⚄ ⚄

LOVE BEGINS IN YOUR HEART

The experience of unconditional love begins in your heart, not in someone else's. Don't make your ability to love yourself conditional on someone else's ability to love you. Your attempt to find love outside yourself always fails, because you cannot receive from another what you haven't been able to give to yourself.

143

⠿ ⠿ ⠿

The Truth about You

When you know the truth about you, you know that you are not your body, although you need to accept it and take care of it. You are not your thoughts and feelings, although you need to be aware of them and see how they are creating the drama of your life. You are not the roles that you are playing—husband or wife, mother or father, son or daughter, employee or boss, secretary or plumber— although you need to make peace with whatever role you choose to play. You are not anything external. You are not anything that can be defined by something or someone else.

144

⚃ ⚅ ⚁

ENLIGHTENMENT

You can't see the light in others until you see it in your-self. Once you see it in yourself, there is no one in whom you do not see the light. It does not matter if they see it or not. You know it's there. And it is the light you address when you speak to them.

145

SOLITUDE

The time you take to integrate your experience is as important as the time you take to have the experience itself.

Every breath has three movements: the inhalation is for taking in experience; the pause is for assimilation; and the exhalation is for the release of experience. While the pause is just a second or two, it is essential for the integrity of the breath.

Solitude allows you to pause. The quality of your life depends upon it. Your energy and enthusiasm arise from it. If you drop out this part, your life will be an empty shell. A great deal may pass in and out of it. But nothing will stick. There will be no assimilation of experience or growth in consciousness.

146

THE FOUNTAINHEAD

The reason that you are looking for love from other people is that you do not realize that love comes only from your own consciousness. It has nothing to do with anyone else.

Don't look to others to provide the love you need. You don't need their love. You need your love.

Love is the only gift you can give yourself. Give it to yourself and the universe resounds with a big "Yes!" Withhold it and the game of hide and seek continues: "looking for love in all the wrong places."

There is only one place you can look for love and find it. No one who has ever looked there has been disappointed.

147

LOVE TAKES NO HOSTAGES

One who loves without conditions places no limits on his freedom nor on anyone else's. He does not try to keep love, for to try to keep it is to lose it.

Love is a gift that must constantly be given as it is asked for in each moment. It takes no hostages, makes no bargains, and cannot be compromised by fear.

148

STAY IN YOUR LIFE

If you want to be kind to others, you need to accept them the way they are and stop judging them or trying to fix their lives.

Don't make rules for other people. Let others find their own way. Support them. Encourage them. Cheer them on. But don't think you know what's good for them. You don't know.

When you stop interfering in the lives of others, you have time to meet your own needs. You stop complaining about the sacrifices you are making for others and get busy accomplishing your own goals.

149

TAKING CARE OF YOURSELF

Nobody comes into embodiment with an empty plate. Everyone has at least a scrap or two to digest.

Your responsibility is to deal with what's on your plate as happily as you can. Don't interfere in the lives of others or you will have a second or a third helping to dispose of.

Practice taking care of yourself and let others do the same. You are not here to do for others what they must do for themselves, nor are other people here to assume responsibilities that belong to you.

FALSE TEACHERS

If you must find a teacher, look for one who empowers you to hear the truth in your own heart. Look for one who loves you without seeking to control you, one who honors you and treats you with dignity and respect.

Do not accept a teacher who tries to make decisions for you or control your life. Do not keep company with those who claim a special knowledge and sell it for a price, those who ask for money or sexual favors in return for spiritual guidance, those who encourage you to give away your power, your self-respect or your dignity. They are false teachers.

151

⚅ ⚀ ⚄

RELIGIOUS RIGHTEOUSNESS

Love is the only door to a spiritual life. Without love, religion offers only dogmas and rigid beliefs. Without love, there is no compassion or charity.

When you judge others, preach to them, or seek to redeem them, you are just projecting your own fear and inadequacy. You are using the words of religion as a substitute for the love you are unable to give or receive.

If you want to follow my teaching, you must learn to look upon all that happens with an open heart and an open mind. Be willing to surrender your narrow beliefs and prejudices. Live your life with loving deeds, not with harsh, unforgiving words.

152

LISTENING WITHIN

You alone know what course of action is best for the fulfillment of your purpose here. But that knowledge is often buried deeply in your heart. Sometimes, it takes a lot of inner listening to connect with your own wisdom. In some cases, connecting to the truth within is not possible until you stop listening to what other people think you should do.

Now it is time to get quiet and turn your attention inward. You can't hear the truth of your heart when your attention is focused on external things. You can best hear the voice of truth within when you put all worries and concerns aside and abide in the silence.

153

ANSWERING THE CALL

The path I have laid out for you is an open one. Anyone who wants to can follow it. No prerequisites are necessary: no baptisms, confessions or communions. Nothing external can prevent you from embracing my teaching.

Yet if you are still holding onto dogma or creeds, if you are convinced that you or anyone else is evil, we cannot step forth together. Thinking that you already have the answers, you may begin to walk, but you will be on a different path.

My path is open to all, yet few choose to follow it. Few are willing to give up what they think they know in order to learn what they know not yet. Many are called, but few answer the call.

154

FINDING THE GOOD

Most teachings make you wrong and come down on you like a sledgehammer. At best, they offer correction; at worst, they condemn you. My teaching is not like that.

I tell you that you are not evil, no matter how many mistakes you have made. I recall you to the truth about yourself. Your challenge is to open your heart to that truth.

You do this by refusing to condemn others, by feeling grateful for the love and nurturing that you have in your life. You focus on what is there, not on what is not there. By finding the good in your life, you reinforce it and extend it to others.

155

Not Condemning

My job is not to condemn, but to understand and to bless. My job is to see the fear in people's eyes and remind them that they are loved. If that is my job, why would I have you beat, burn or excommunicate those who are most in need of your love? Please, do not put your words in my mouth and attribute them to me.

You have misunderstood. You are mistaken. My teaching is about love, not about judgment, condemnation, or punishment.

156

Two Rules

I have given you only two rules: to love God and to love one another. Those are the only rules you need. Do not ask me for more. Do not ask me to take sides in your soap opera battles. Am I pro-life or pro-choice? How could I be one without also being the other?

When the truth comes to you, you no longer need to attack your brother. Even if you think you are right and he is wrong, you will not attack him with "the truth," but offer him your understanding and your support.

Every time I give a teaching, someone makes it into a stick to beat people with. Please, my friends, words that are used to beat people up cannot come from me.

157

WORDS AND DEEDS

If you would serve this teaching, please learn it first. Demonstrate it in your life through your loving thoughts and actions.

Do not pretend to be what you are not. Do not be a mouthpiece for words and beliefs you have not brought fully into the rhythms of your life.

All who extend my teaching do so from the same level of consciousness as me. Otherwise what they extend cannot be my teaching.

158

EQUALITY FOR ALL

Women have an equal place in my church. They have always had that place and will always have it. Those who deny women their rightful place in the community are not following my teaching.

Gays and lesbians, blacks, Asians, Hispanics, born-agains, fundamentalists, Buddhists, Jews, lawyers and politicians all have a place in the community of faith. Everyone is welcome. No one should be excluded, and all who participate in the community should have the opportunity to serve in leadership positions.

My teaching has never been exclusive or hierarchical. It has never given preference to one person over another. It is a teaching of uncompromising and absolute equality.

159

Making Amends

It is not too late for you to learn from your mistakes and make amends to those whom you have injured or judged unfairly. Your mistakes do not condemn you unless you insist on holding onto them.

Let them go. You can grow. You can change. You can be wiser than you once were. You can stop being a mouthpiece for fear and become a spokesperson for forgiveness and love.

160

THE BOTTOMLESS WELL

Your heart is the place where love is born. It is the bottomless well from which you can draw as often as you need to. Every time you come to the well, you drink the waters of life. Your spiritual thirst is quenched. Your sins are forgiven. You are baptized, healed and renewed.

Whenever life feels difficult, there is only one place that offers you sanctuary. You must learn to make your pilgrimage there on a regular basis.

161

ENLIGHTENMENT FOR SALE

No one has anything to give you that you do not already have. Those who promise you miracles, spiritual powers, or enlightenment have nothing to offer you. They are just lining their pockets at your expense. They cannot bring you freedom from suffering. Only you can do that.

Be realistic about your experience here. There is only one person who needs to wake up and that is you.

Those who have a gift to give you will not withhold it. Those who withhold information or love from you, have no gift to give.

Do not tolerate the idea that salvation lies somewhere else. It doesn't.

162

Other People's Rules

If you allow it, people will be only too glad to prescribe for you and take your freedom away. Don't live by other people's rules. With good humor, let go of relationships with people who would tell you what to think or what to do.

163

Awareness

Awareness is not a gift, but a gesture of the self, an energetic movement to be present and embrace life. Simply desire to be aware and awareness is. It comes and goes with the breath. Breathe in to embrace this moment. Breathe out to release it. Each breath is an act of awareness.

164

∷ ∙ ∷

TELLING THE TRUTH

Abuse and betrayal happen when plans are held rigidly or agreements are broken in fear. If you make a commitment and don't feel comfortable keeping it, it is your responsibility to communicate this to the people involved. At all times, you best honor others by telling the truth about your experience.

165

AMBIVALENCE

To say "yes" or "no" to another person is a clear communication. But to say "no" and mean "yes" or to say
"yes" and mean "no" creates the conditions for abuse.

⚃ ⚃ ⚄

Saying No to the False

Need I remind you that commitment to the truth is not popular? Often it means saying "yes" when others would say "no," or saying "no" when others would say "yes."

Many of you cannot imagine that saying "no" can be a loving act. Yet if your child puts his hand on a hot stove, you say "no" quickly and firmly. You do not want him to hurt himself. And then you put your arm around him and reassure him that you love him.

How many times does your brother come to you with his hand on the stove? You cannot support behavior that you know will be hurtful to another person. And you don't want your friends to support that kind of behavior in you.

167

CIVIL DISOBEDIENCE

My crucifixion was an act of civil disobedience. I accepted torture and death, because I refused to speak anything but the truth that I knew in my heart.

To stand for the truth in the face of opposition is not an easy thing to do. If one values one's body too much, one cannot do it. Only one who values the truth above all else can put himself in harm's way for the sake of what he believes in.

168

⠿ ⠿ ⠿

Non-Violence

Standing up for truth is a forceful act, but it is not a violent one. One who stands for truth must do so in a loving way or it is not truth s/he stands for.

There will be times when you must stand up for yourself and for others who are being mistreated. You cannot live your life in a state of fear, cowering in a corner while others make decisions for you. You must stand up and be counted.

But please do so lovingly, compassionately, respectfully. Do it knowing that there is no enemy out there. Each brother or sister, no matter how angry, fearful or distraught, deserves your support and your respect.

169

LEAVE YOUR NETS

There comes a time in life when the fisherman must leave his nets, a time when you must listen to your inner voice and follow it, even when other people object. Sometimes, you have to leave your home, your school, your job, and your religion to see beyond the narrow conditions that define your life. Then, you know that you are not just a son or a daughter, a husband or a wife, a carpenter or a plumber, a black person or a white person, a Christian or a Jew. You discover the Essence within you that transcends all the roles that you play and all the labels placed upon you.

170

STANDING IN THE TRUTH

I have asked you to stand alone, not because I wish to isolate you, but so you can know the truth and anchor in it. For there will be times when you will be asked to stand in that truth in the midst of a crowd of people who condemn you as they once condemned me. There will be times when you too will be the voice in the wilderness that helps people find their way back home.

171

LOVE, TRUTH AND ESSENCE

To discover love, truth, and essence, you must refuse to be satisfied with their imitations. If you accept conditional love, you will not experience love without conditions. If you accept any form of dogma, judgment or prejudice, you will not know the pure truth of the heart. If you seek the approval of other men and women, you will not express your essential Self even when it is called for.

When you speak of love, please ask "Is my love free of conditions?" When you speak of truth, ask "Is my truth free of judgment or opinion?" When you speak of essence, ask "Am I attached to the way people perceive or receive me?"

172

⚅ ⚅ ⚅

FREEDOM TO BE YOURSELF

Freedom to be yourself requires more detachment than you think. As long as you want something from anyone, you cannot be yourself. Only when you want nothing in particular from anyone are you free to be yourself and to interact honestly and authentically with others.

173

⚃ ⚄ ⚄

TRUSTING THE SOURCE

Trust in your connection to the Source of all things. You have everything you need to be guided wisely in your life. You are no further away from God than I am. You don't need me to bring you to the feet of the Divine. You are already there.

God is incapable of moving away from you. When you do not feel the presence, it is because you have moved away. You have given your power to some earthly authority. You have left the place of the indwelling God in search of something special in the world.

174

TEACHERS WHO EMPOWER

If you have a teacher who empowers you, I am happy. It does not matter to me if that teacher is a Buddhist or a Jew, a Christian or a Muslim, a shaman or a businessman. If you are learning to trust yourself and become more open in your mind and your heart, then I am happy for you. It does not matter what specific path you are on, what symbols you believe in, or what scrolls you consider sacred. I look to the fruit of those beliefs to see if you are stepping into your divinity or giving that power away to someone else.

Choose a teacher who empowers you and you will discover truth within your own heart. When you give your power away, to me or to anyone else, I know that you have not heard me.

175

THE NEXT STEP

Your path has its own simple beauty and mystery. It is never what you think it is. Yet it is never beyond your ability to intuit the next step.

WHO IS GOD?

You prepare the inner temple for God to come. And who, my friends, is God but the One in you who knows and understands, the One who loves and accepts you without conditions, under all circumstances, now and for all time?

That being is not outside of you, but in your heart of hearts. When you ask sincerely, this is the One who answers. When you knock, this is the One who opens the door.

THE CALL TO AWAKEN

Deeply imbedded in your psyche is the call to awaken. It does not sound like the call that anyone else hears. If you are listening to others, you will not hear the call within your own heart.

But once you hear it, you will recognize that others hear it too in their own way. And you will be able to join with them in simple support. Blessing them, you bless yourself. Setting them free to travel their own path, you will set yourself free to travel yours.

178

THE BODY

The body is not bad or inferior in any way. It is simply temporal. You will never find ultimate meaning by satisfying its needs or by denying those needs.

The body is a means. It is a vehicle for gathering experience. It has a purpose.

Please do not disrespect or demean your body. On the other hand, do not make your body into a god that you worship.

When you enjoy and care for your body, it can serve you better. But no body is perfect. All bodies eventually break down. Bodies are not meant to last forever.

Some things are temporary and temporal, and some are eternal. The body is not eternal. The best it can be is a temporary servant.

179

⚃ ⚄ ⚄

SEX WITHOUT LOVE

The only sexual expression that is reprehensible is sex without love. Some people try to find satisfaction through the pleasure of orgasm. This never works, because after the peak of every orgasm is the trough of existential contact with the partner. If you love the person you are with, the trough will be a peaceful, comforting space. If you do not love the person, the trough will feel hollow.

Sex without love is ultimately unsatisfactory and addictive. More will always be needed: more sex, more partners, more stimulation. But more is never enough. Sex without love, under any guise, fragments the energy of your union and exacerbates your emotional wounds.

⚅ ⚅ ⚅

THE EGO

Your ego is the part of you that doesn't know that you are loved. It can't give love, because it doesn't know it has love to give.

When you compassionately accept your ego and the ego of others, consciousness relaxes. Resistance ceases to be. As soon as ego recognizes it is loved, it ceases to be ego.

Ego must die as ego to be reborn as love. The unlimited, eternal Self is not born until the limited, temporal self dies.

181

SEXUAL LOVE

Physical love is no less beautiful than other forms of love, nor can it be separated from them. Those who view physical love as unholy will experience it that way, not because it is, but because they perceive it that way.

In a spiritual relationship, the urge to sexual union becomes a way of connecting emotionally with one's partner. Sexual passion becomes part of a full-chakra embrace, one element of an overall attraction to the beloved.

DYING

Dying is one of the best ways to learn to be present. When you are dying, you are aware of things in a way you never were before. You notice every breath, every nuance, every flower, every word or gesture of love.

Dying is like a crash course in waking up. Now that doesn't mean that each person who dies wakes up. It just means s/he has taken the course.

Disengaging from meaningless identity is an inevitable aspect of the path back home. The less attachment you have to the past, the more blissful your experience becomes.

183

DEATH AND REBIRTH

I have told you that unless you die and be reborn you cannot enter the kingdom of heaven. No one comes here to earth without suffering the pain of loss. Every identity you assume will be taken from you and every person you love will die. It is just a matter of time.

All sacred teachings exhort you not to be attached to the things of this world, because they are not permanent. Yet you get attached nonetheless. That is part of the process of your awakening: getting attached and letting go; embracing and releasing. In this way, love is deepened and wisdom is born.

184

A PROFOUND PEACE

You will experience many small deaths in the course of your life, many times when you must let go of the arms that once comforted you and walk alone into the uncertain future. Every time you do so your fears will rise up and you will have to walk through them.

Don't be impatient. Awakening is a process. The tide goes out and comes back in. People let go of one attachment only to form another one that challenges them more. Life is rhythmic, but progressive.

As earth and water breathe together, the shape of the beach changes. Storms come and go, but in the end a profound peace pervades the heart and mind, a deep acceptance and a quiet recognition that all things are perfect as they are.

185

Love is Without Form

Permanence cannot be found at the level of form. All form is a manifestation of the original formlessness of the universe. What is all-inclusive, all-accepting, all-loving cannot be limited to form.

Love is without conditions; that it to say it is without form.

186

THE DEATH OF THE EGO

You cannot avoid the death of the ego, nor can you avoid the death of the body. But these are not necessarily the same. Do not make the mistake of believing that your ego dies when your body does, or that your body dies when your ego does.

187

ASCENSION

When you act in a loving way and speak loving words, the Spirit dwells in you and is awakened in others. Then you are the light of the world, and physical reality does not seem as dense as it was before. This is the correct meaning of the word ascension.

When love is present, the body and the world are lifted up. They are infused with light, possibility and celebration of goodness. The world you see when Spirit is present in your heart and your life is not the same world that you see when you are preoccupied with your ego needs.

188

THE PRESENCE OF LOVE

Only the presence of Love is real. Everything else is an illusion.

189

A LIFE OF SERVICE

As soon as you begin to see that your needs are the same as the needs of others, the veil begins to lift. You stop needing special treatment. You stop giving others special treatment. What you want for one, you want for all.

The perception of equality is the beginning of the transcendence of the body and the physical world. When you no longer hold yourself separate from others, you can serve without being attached. You can give without needing to know how the gift is being received.

190

LOVE HAPPENS NOW

When love is present, you don't worry about the future. When love is lacking, then you want guarantees about tomorrow.

Love comes into being right now. The alpha and omega of existence are present in this moment. There will never be more love than is possible here and now.

Do you hear that? The greatest love that you can attain is attainable right now. It cannot be experienced in the past or future.

191

HEAVEN IS HERE

You forgive not to gain salvation in the future, but to experience salvation right here, right now.

Your entire spirituality is lived in this moment only. It has nothing to do with anything you have ever thought or felt in the past. It is happening right now, with the circumstance that lies before you.

192

GRATITUDE

You experience scarcity only when you find fault with the situation you are presented with in the moment. When you see the situation and feel gratitude for it, you experience only abundance and bliss.

193

In the Present Moment

Happiness occurs only in the present moment. If you become concerned about whether you will be happy tomorrow or even five minutes from now, you won't be able to be happy now. Your scheming and dreaming take you away from your present happiness.

Please take a deep breath and come back into your heart. All of the chaos and confusion in your mind can be transcended through your simple decision to be wholly present and attentive right now. That is the miraculous truth.

194

FREEDOM FROM THE PAST

I have told you that you are free to live whatever life you choose to live. "Fat chance!" you say, pointing to the chains on your feet.

"Who made those chains?" I ask.

"God did!" you angrily exclaim.

"No. It is not true. God did not make the chains. If He made them, you would never escape from the prison of your own beliefs."

195

CENTERING

The more attached you are to the past, or the more invested you are in a future outcome, the harder it is for you to accept "what is" and work with it.

To be in the present, you need to stay centered in what you know and put the past and the future aside. For example, you don't know that the past is going to repeat itself. Old patterns may dissolve or they may reappear. You don't know. You know only how you feel about what is happening right now.

If you can stay with this, then you can be honest with yourself and others. You can say what you are able to commit to now and what you are not ready to promise.

Things may change in the future, but you can't live right now hoping they are going to change. You must be where you are, not where you want to be.

196

PAST LIVES

If memories of the past come up, simply acknowledge them. Do this not to empower the past, but to complete it, so that you can be present now. Anything that takes you away from your immediate communion with life is not helpful.

Once the past is integrated, it no longer troubles you. Remember the question: if a tree falls in the forest and nobody hears it, did it make a sound? The answer is no. Without an experiencer, there is no experience.

Are there past lives? Only if you remember them. And if you remember them, you will continue to live them until you come to forgiveness of yourself and the others involved.

197

Dancing with the Past

Do not gather wood unless you want to make a fire. Do not stir the pot unless you want to smell the stew. Do not solicit the past unless you want to dance with it.

But if there is a fire in your house, you must pick up your things and leave. If the stew is boiling, you can't help but smell it. If the past is dancing in your mirror, you can't pretend to be in samadhi.

Resistance of experience creates endless detours. But so does seeking.

Do not resist. Do not seek. Just deal with what comes up as it arises.

198

EMPTYING THE CUP

When you are attached to what you already have, how can you bring in anything new in? To bring in something new, fresh and unpredictable, you must surrender something old, stale and habitual.

If the cup is full of old, cold tea, you cannot pour new, hot tea into it. First you have to empty the cup. Then you can fill it.

199

⚃ · ⚅

CLOSED DOORS

Please, don't try to walk through closed doors. You will hurt yourself unnecessarily. Even if you don't know why a door is closed, at least respect the fact that it is. And don't struggle with the doorknob. If the door were open, you would know it.

Much of the pain in your life happens when you attempt to walk through closed doors or try to put square pegs in round holes. You try to hold onto someone who is ready to go, or you try to get somebody to do something before s/he is ready.

Stop trying to control what happens. Instead, accept what is and work with it. Swimming with the current is far easier than swimming upstream.

200

INTERFERENCE

When you interfere with what is, you create strife for yourself and others. You trespass. You get in the way.

When you know that things are not flowing, you need to step back and realize that your actions are not helpful. You need to stop, pause, and consider. That way you won't make the situation worse than it is.

When you interfere in the natural order of things, there is suffering. As soon as you stop interfering, suffering stops.

201

INTERNAL SHIFTS

What you love and give your full attention to prospers. Withdraw your love and attention and a shift will occur.

When you cease to be committed to a job or a relationship, it begins to fall apart. Your lack of caring and investment of positive energy in the job or relationship will alienate others or make them feel insecure and needy.

You can blame this change on your spouse or your boss, but you will be missing the whole point. The relationship or job no longer works because you are no longer giving it your love, your support, and your commitment.

The Fire of Change

There is always some degree of pain in the release of someone or something that once brought you joy and happiness. You have to be patient and mourn the loss. But when your mourning is over, you will see things differently. Opportunities you never could have dreamed of will come into your life.

As the old dies, the new is born. The phoenix rises from the ashes of destruction.

The fire of change is never easy to weather. But if you surrender, the conflagration is quickly over. In the enriched soil, the seeds of tomorrow can be sown.

203

⚅ ⚅ ⚅

YOUR ANGELIC NATURE

Angels are not seven-foot tall creatures with wings. They are beings who have learned to honor themselves. Because they have walked through the door, they can hold the door open for you.

Don't see angels outside of yourself. That is not where they will be found. They live in a dimension that you can touch only with your heart.

PATIENCE

When one door is closed, you must wait patiently for another door to open. As long as you forgive yourself and others, you won't have to wait long.

It isn't helpful to obsess about your mistakes. Guilt doesn't help you act more responsibly toward others. Correct your mistakes if you can. Make amends to those you have hurt. But, if there is nothing you can do to make the situation better, then just accept it as it is. Sometimes, there's nothing to be done. It's no one's fault.

In knowing that life is okay, no matter how ragged and unfinished it seems, there is room for movement. A shift can happen. A door that was closed just moments ago may spontaneously open.

205

THE DOOR TO YOUR HEART

The most important door is the one to your heart. If it is open, then the whole universe abides in you. If it is closed, then you stand alone against the world.

A heart in resistance gets tired quickly. Life weighs heavily upon it. But a heart that is open is filled with energy. It dances and sings.

When the door to your heart is open, all the important doors open in the world. You go where you need to go. Nothing interferes with your purpose or your destiny.

⊠ ⊡ ⊞

The Dance of Acceptance

Acceptance is a life-long dance. You get better at it the more you do it. But you never dance perfectly. Fear and resistance continue to come up and you do the best you can with them.

In the dance of acceptance, unconscious becomes conscious. Your fear becomes your partner.

The unhappier you are, the harder the dance becomes, because you must dance with your unhappiness. But even your unhappiness can be accepted. There is nothing you cannot dance with if only you are willing.

THE POETRY OF BEING

The simple beauty and majesty of life is to be found in its cyclical rhythms: the rising and setting of the sun, the phases of the moon, the changes in the seasons, the beating of the heart, the rhythmic unfolding of the breath. Repetition provides continuity, familiarity, and safety.

It is not just the reach of your hands toward the sky, but the rootedness of your feet in the ground that helps you bring heaven to earth. Spirituality is a living with, as well as a living for. It is the poetry of being, the rhythm of life unfolding in each person and each relationship, moment to moment.

208

⚃ ⚄ ⚅

WHEN THE SNOW FALLS

When the snow falls, it covers ground, plants, trees, houses and roads with a white mantle. Everything looks fresh, new, innocent. Forgiveness comes in the same way, undoing the grievances of the past, replacing judgments with acceptance. In the light of forgiveness, you see your problems and challenges differently. You feel capable of meeting your life just the way it is.

Forgiveness is as far-reaching as the snow. It touches everything in your life. But for forgiveness to bless you, you must be willing to receive it, as the ground receives the snowfall. You must be willing to be occupied and cleansed by something greater than your limited sense of self.

209

FORGIVENESS

As hard as you try to avoid hurting your brother, he continues to cry out in pain. Your fear is triggered by his fear and vice versa.

Forgiveness helps you find a way to soften and come together with another person when you feel angry or hurt. It helps you surrender your need to be right and to make the other person wrong.

Intimacy with others is not possible unless you can forgive the offenses and hurts of the past. When you forgive, you help your relationships develop the resiliency they need to survive long-term.

⚅ ⚅ ⚅

The Beloved Appears

When you have faithfully answered the call for love within your own heart, the Beloved appears unannounced on your doorstep. This is not a magical formula, but the fruit of a committed spiritual practice.

211

COMPASSION

There is no permanence in the world. Fame and ignominy, poverty and riches, happiness and despair run hand in hand. You can't experience one side without experiencing the other.

Pain is the great equalizer. It brings you to your knees. It makes you more humble and sensitive to the needs of others.

If you have touched your own pain deeply, you feel compassion when you see others in pain. You do not need to push them away, nor do you need to try to fix them. You just hold them deeply in your heart. You offer them a hug and some words of encouragement. You know what they are going through.

212

You are the Sentinel

Pain is a doorway you walk through when you are ready. Until then, you are the doorkeeper, the sentinel who decides whom to exclude and whom to let in.

It is okay not to be ready. It's okay to exclude people or situations that feel unsafe. You are in charge of your own healing process. You decide how fast to go. Don't let anyone else dictate the pace of your healing process.

Others may have ideas, suggestions, or plans for you. Thank them for their concern, but be clear with them that you, not they, are making the decisions in your life.

213

TRUSTING THE PROCESS

You don't need to have all the answers to grow, to walk through your fears, to inhabit your life fully. As you tell your story and witness to the stories of others, the alchemical process of transformation begins in your heart. And *It*, not you or I, is in charge of the journey.

I cannot tell you where the journey will take you. Indeed, it is not important for you to know. But I can tell you to trust the process and know that it is bringing you home to your true Self, home to the most profound intimacy, home to your eternal connection with the divine.

214

⊞ ⊞ ⊞

THE POTTER & THE CLAY

The potter is not defined by the clay but by what s/he chooses to do with it.

The clay gets molded by your willingness to stay in your process. Through your struggle and surrender, the work of art is offered, torn apart and offered once again. At some point, you know it is finished and you can work on it no more. And then you walk away from it and more clay is given into your hands. It has a different consistency, a different potential. It brings new challenges.

Just being in your life is the molding process. Even when it seems that you are resisting your life, the clay is being worked. You can't be alive and not be engaged in the process of creation.

215

THE DREAMER AWAKENS

You are the dreamer of the darkness and the one who brings the light. You are the tempter and the savior rolled into one. This you will come to know if you don't know it already.

216

KNOCK AND THE DOOR WILL OPEN

I have told you that—no matter how many times you have refused to enter the sanctuary—you have only to knock and the door will be opened to you. I have said to you "Ask, and it shall be given you," but you refuse to believe me. You think that someone is counting your sins, your moments of indecision or recalcitrance, but it is not true. You are the only one counting.

I say to you, brother and sister, "Stop counting; stop making excuses; stop pretending that the door is locked. I am here at the threshold. Reach out and take my hand and we will open the door and walk through together."

I am the door to love without conditions. When you walk through, you too will be the door.

List of Divinatory Responses

Paul Ferrini's unique blend of radical Christianity and other wisdom traditions, goes beyond self-help and recovery into the heart of healing. He is the author of twenty-one books including his latest books *I am the Door, Reflections of the Christ Mind* and *The Way of Peace*. His Christ Mind Series includes the bestseller *Love Without Conditions, The Silence of the Heart, Miracle of Love* and *Return to the Garden*. Other recent books include *The Seven Spiritual Laws of Relationship, Grace Unfolding, Living in the Heart, Crossing the Water, The Ecstatic Moment* and *Waking Up Together*.

Paul Ferrini is the founder and editor of *Miracles Magazine* and a nationally known teacher and workshop leader. His conferences, retreats, and Affinity Group Process have helped thousands of people deepen their practice of forgiveness and open their hearts to the divine presence in themselves and others. For more information on Paul's workshops and retreats or The Affinity Group Process, contact Heartways Press, P.O. Box 99, Greenfield, MA 01302-0099 or call 413-774-9474.

BOOKS AND TAPES
AVAILABLE FROM HEARTWAYS PRESS

I am the Door

I AM THE DOOR
by Paul Ferrini
ISBN 1-879159-41-4
288 pages hardcover
$21.95

Years ago, Paul Ferrini began hearing a persistent inner voice that said "I want you to acknowledge me." He also had a series of dreams in which Jesus appeared to teach him. Later, when Ferrini's relationship with his teacher was firmly established, the four books in the *Reflections of the Christ Mind* series were published. Here, in this lovely lyrical collection, we can hear the voice of Jesus speaking directly to us about practical topics of everyday life that our close to our hearts like work and livelihood, relationships, community, forgiveness, spiritual practices, and miracles.

When you put this book down, there will no doubt in your mind that the teachings of the master are alive today. Your life will never be the same.

The Way of Peace
A System of Guidance for
Connecting with the Christ Within

Paul Ferrini

New

THE WAY OF PEACE
by Paul Ferrini
ISBN 1-879159-42-2
256 pages hardcover
$19.95

The Way of Peace is a simple method for connecting with the wisdom and truth that lie within our hearts. The two hundred and sixteen oracular messages in this book were culled from the bestselling *Reflections of the Christ Mind* series by Paul Ferrini.

Open this little book spontaneously to receive inspirational guidance, or ask a formal question and follow the simple divinatory procedure described in the introduction. You will be amazed at the depth and the accuracy of the response you receive.

Like the *I-Ching, the Book of Runes*, and other systems of guidance, *The Way of Peace* empowers you to connect with peace within and act in harmony with your true self and the unique circumstances of your life.

Special dice, blessed by the author, are available for using *The Way of Peace* as an oracle. To order these dice, send $3.00 plus shipping.

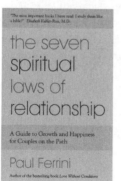

"The most important books I have read. I study them like a bible." Elisabeth Kübler-Ross, M.D.

the seven
spiritual
laws of
relationship

A Guide to Growth and Happiness
for Couples on the Path

Paul Ferrini

Author of the bestselling book Love Without Conditions

The Relationship Book You've Been Waiting For

THE SEVEN SPIRITUAL LAWS OF RELATIONSHIP: A GUIDE TO GROWTH AND HAPPINESS FOR COUPLES ON THE PATH
144 pages paperback $10.95
ISBN 1-879159-39-2

This simple but profound guide to growth and happiness for couples will help you and your partner:

- Make a realistic commitment to each other
- Develop a shared experience that nurtures your relationship
- Give each other the space to grow and express yourselves as individuals
- Communicate by listening without judgment and telling the truth in a non-blaming way
- Understand how you mirror each other
- Stop blaming your partner and take responsibility for your thoughts, feelings and actions
- Practice forgiveness together on an ongoing basis

These seven spiritual principles will help you weather the ups and downs of your relationship so that you and your partner can grow together and deepen the intimacy between you. The book also includes a special section on living alone and preparing to be in relationship and a section on separating with love when a relationship needs to change form or come to completion.

Our Surrender Invites Grace

GRACE UNFOLDING: THE ART OF LIVING
A SURRENDERED LIFE
96 pages paperback $9.95
ISBN 1-879159-37-6

As we surrender to the truth of our being, we learn to relinquish the need to control our lives, figure things out, or predict the future. We begin to let go of our judgments and interpretations and accept life the way it is. When we can be fully present with whatever life brings, we are guided to take the next step on our journey. That is the way that grace unfolds in our lives.

RETURN TO THE GARDEN
REFLECTIONS OF THE CHRIST MIND,
PART IV
$12.95, Paperback
ISBN 1-879159-35-X

"In the Garden, all our needs were provided for. We knew no struggle or hardship. We were God's beloved. But happiness was not enough for us. We wanted the freedom to live our own lives. To evolve, we had to learn to become love-givers, not just love-receivers.

We all know what happened then. We were cast out of the Garden and for the first time in our lives we felt shame, jealousy, anger, lack. We experienced highs and lows, joy and sorrow. Our lives became difficult. We had to work hard to survive. We had to make mistakes and learn from them.

Initially, we tried to blame others for our mistakes. But that did not make our lives any easier. It just deepened our pain and misery. We had to learn to face our fears, instead of projecting them onto each other.

Returning to the Garden, we are different than we were when we left hellbent on expressing our creativity at any cost. We return humble and sensitive to the needs of all. We return not just as created, but as co-creator, not just as son of man, but also as son of God."

*Learn the Spiritual Practice Associated
with the Christ Mind Teachings*

LIVING IN THE HEART THE AFFINITY PROCESS AND THE
PATH OF UNCONDITIONAL LOVE AND ACCEPTANCE

Paperback $10.95
ISBN 1-879159-36-8

The long awaited, definitive book on the *Affinity Process* is finally here. For years, the *Affinity Process* has been refined by participants so that it could be easily understood and experienced. Now, you can learn how to hold a safe, loving, non-judgmental space for yourself and others which will enable you to open your heart and move through your fears. The *Affinity Process* will help you learn to take responsibility for your fears and judgments so that you won't project them onto others. It will help you learn to listen deeply and without judgment to others. And it will teach you how to tell your truth clearly without blaming others for your experience.

Part One contains an in-depth description of the principles on which the *Affinity Process* is based. Part Two contains a detailed discussion of the *Affinity Group Guidelines*. And Part Three contains a manual for people who wish to facilitate an *Affinity Group* in their community.

If you are a serious student of the *Christ Mind* teachings, this book is essential for you. It will enable you to begin a spiritual practice which will transform your life and the lives of others. It will also offer you a way of extending the teachings of love and forgiveness throughout your community.

LOVE WITHOUT CONDITIONS,

REFLECTIONS OF THE CHRIST MIND, PART I
by Paul Ferrini
The Book on Tape Read by the Author
2 Cassettes, Approximately 3.25 hours
ISBN 1-879159-24-4 $19.95

Now on audio tape: the incredible book from Jesus calling us to awaken to our own Christhood. Listen to this gentle, profound book while driving in your car or before going to sleep at night. Elisabeth Kubler-Ross calls this "the most important book I have read. I study it like a Bible." Find out for yourself how this amazing book has helped thousands of people understand the radical teachings of Jesus and begin to integrate these teachings into their lives.

With its heartfelt combination of sensuality and spirituality, Paul Ferrini's poetry has been compared to the poetry of Rumi.

CROSSING THE WATER:

POEMS ABOUT HEALING

AND FORGIVENESS IN

OUR RELATIONSHIPS

The time for healing and reconciliation has come, Ferrini writes. Our relationships help us heal childhood wounds, walk through our deepest fears, and cross over the water of our emotional pain. Just as the rocks in the river are pounded and caressed to rounded stone, the rough edges of our personalities are worn smooth in the context of a committed relationship. If we can keep our hearts open, we can heal together, experience genuine equality, and discover what it means to give and receive love without conditions.

With its heartfelt combination of sensuality and spirituality, Paul Ferrini's poetry has been compared to the poetry of Rumi. These luminous poems demonstrate why Paul Ferrini is first a poet, a lover and a mystic. Come to this feast of the beloved with an open heart and open ears. 96 pp. paper ISBN 1-879159-25-2 $9.95.

MIRACLE OF LOVE: REFLECTIONS OF THE CHRIST MIND, PART III

In this volume of the Christ Mind series, Jesus sets the record straight regarding a number of events in his life. He tells us: "I was born to a simple woman in a barn. She was no more a virgin than your mother was." Moreover, the virgin birth was not the only myth surrounding his life and teaching. So were the concepts of vicarious atonement and physical resurrection.

Relentlessly, the master tears down the rigid dogma and hierarchical teachings that obscure his simple message of love and forgiveness. He encourages us to take him down from the pedestal and the cross and see him as an equal brother who found the way out of suffering by opening his heart totally. We too can open our hearts and find peace and happiness. "The power of love will make miracles in your life as wonderful as any attributed to me," he tells us. "Your birth into this embodiment is no less holy than mine. The love that you extend to others is no less important than the love I extend to you." 192 pp. paper ISBN 1-879159-23-6 $12.95.

There comes a time for all of us when the outer destinations no longer satisfy and we finally understand that the love and happiness we seek cannot be found outside of us. It must be found in our own hearts, on the other side of our pain. "The Road to Nowhere is the path through your heart. It is not a journey of escape. It is a journey through your pain to end the pain of separation."

This book makes it clear that we can no longer rely on outer teachers or teachings to find our spiritual identity. Nor can we find who we are in relationships where boundaries are blurred and one person makes decisions for another. If we want to be authentic, we can't allow anyone else to be an authority for us, nor can we allow ourselves to be an authority for another person.

Authentic relationships happen between equal partners who take responsibility for their own consciousness and experience. When their buttons are pushed, they are willing to look at the obstacles they have erected to the experience of love and acceptance. As they understand and surrender the false ideas and emotional reactions that create separation, genuine intimacy becomes possible, and the sacred dimension of the relationship is born. 216 pp. paper ISBN 1-879159-17-1 $14.95

THE ECSTATIC MOMENT: A PRACTICAL MANUAL FOR OPENING YOUR HEART AND STAYING IN IT.

A simple, power-packed guide that helps us take appropriate responsibility for our experience and establish healthy boundaries with others. Part II contains many helpful exercises and meditations that teach us to stay centered, clear and open in heart and mind. The Affinity Group Process and other group practices help us learn important listening and communication skills that can transform our troubled relationships. Once you have read this book, you will keep it in your briefcase or on your bedside table, referring to it often. You will not find a more practical, down to earth guide to contemporary spirituality. You will want to order copies for all your friends. 128 pp. paper   ISBN 1-879159-18-X $10.95

THE SILENCE OF THE HEART: REFLECTIONS OF THE CHRIST MIND, PART II

A powerful sequel to *Love Without Conditions*. John Bradshaw says: "with deep insight and sparkling clarity, this book demonstrates that the roots of all abuse are to be found in our own self-betrayal. Paul Ferrini leads us skillfully and courageously beyond shame, blame, and attachment to our wounds into the depths of self-forgiveness...a must read for all people who are ready to take responsibility for their own healing." 218 pp. paper. ISBN 1-879159-16-3 $14.95

LOVE WITHOUT CONDITIONS: REFLECTIONS OF THE CHRIST MIND, PART I

An incredible book from Jesus calling us to awaken to our Christhood. Rarely has any book conveyed the teachings of the master in such a simple but profound manner. This book will help you to bring your understanding from the head to the heart so that you can model the teachings of love and forgiveness in your daily life. 192 pp. paper ISBN 1-879159-15-5 $12.00

THE WISDOM OF THE SELF

This ground-breaking book explores our authentic experience and our journey to wholeness. "Your life is your spiritual path. Don't be quick to abandon it for promises of bigger and better experiences. You are getting exactly the experiences you need to grow. If your growth seems too slow or uneventful for you, it is because you have not fully embraced the situations and relationships at hand...To know the Self is to allow everything, to embrace the totality of who we are, all that we think and feel, all of our fear, all of our love." 229 pp. paper ISBN 1-879159-14-7 $12.00

THE TWELVE STEPS OF FORGIVENESS

A practical manual for healing ourselves and our relationships. This book gives us a step-by-step process for moving through our fears, projections, judgments, and guilt so that we can take responsibility for creating the life we want. With great gentleness, we learn to embrace our lessons and to find equality with others. A must read for all in recovery and others seeking spiritual wholeness. 128 pp. paper ISBN 1-879159-10-4 $10.00

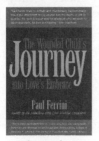

THE WOUNDED CHILD'S JOURNEY: INTO LOVE'S EMBRACE

This book explores a healing process in which we confront our deep-seated guilt and fear, bringing love and forgiveness to the wounded child within. By surrendering our judgments of self and others, we overcome feelings of separation and dismantle co-dependent patterns that restrict our self-expression and ability to give and receive love. 225pp. paper ISBN 1-879159-06-6 $12.00

THE BRIDGE TO REALITY

A Heart-Centered Approach to *A Course in Miracles* and the Process of Inner Healing. Sharing his experiences of spiritual awakening, Paul emphasizes self-acceptance and forgiveness as cornerstones of spiritual practice. Presented with beautiful photos, this book conveys the essence of *The Course* as it is lived in daily life. 192 pp. paper ISBN 1-879159-03-1 $12.00

FROM EGO TO SELF

108 illustrated affirmations designed to offer you a new way of viewing conflict situations so that you can overcome negative thinking and bring more energy, faith and optimism into your life. 144 pp. paper ISBN 1-879159-01-5 $10.00

VIRTUES OF THE WAY

A lyrical work of contemporary scripture reminiscent of the *Tao Te Ching*. Beautifully illustrated, this inspirational book will help you cultivate the spiritual values required to fulfill your creative purpose and live in harmony with others. 64 pp. paper ISBN 1-879159-02-3 $7.50

THE BODY OF TRUTH

A crystal clear introduction to the universal teachings of love and forgiveness. This book traces all forms of suffering to negative attitudes and false beliefs, which we have the ability to transform. 64 pp. paper ISBN 1-879159-02-3 $7.50

AVAILABLE LIGHT

Inspirational, passionate poems dealing with the work of inner integration, love and relationships, death and re-birth, loss and abundance, life purpose and the reality of spiritual vision. 128 pp. paper ISBN 1-879159-05-8 $12.00

THE POETRY OF THE SOUL

With its heartfelt combination of sensuality and spirituality, Paul Ferrini's poetry has been compared to the poetry of Rumi. These luminous poems read by the author demonstrate why Paul Ferrini is first a poet, a lover and a mystic. Come to this feast of the beloved with an open heart and open ears. With Suzi Kesler on piano. $10.00 ISBN 1-879159-26-0

THE CIRCLE OF HEALING

The meditation and healing tape that many of you have been seeking. This gentle meditation opens the heart to love's presence and extends that love to all the beings in your experience. A powerful tape with inspirational piano accompaniment by Michael Gray. ISBN 1-879159-08-2 $10.00

HEALING THE WOUNDED CHILD

A potent healing tape that accesses old feelings of pain, fragmentation, self-judgment and separation and brings them into the light of conscious awareness and acceptance. Side two includes a hauntingly beautiful "inner child" reading from The Bridge to Reality with piano accompaniment by Michael Gray. ISBN 1-879159-11-2 $10.00

FORGIVENESS: RETURNING TO THE ORIGINAL BLESSING

A self healing tape that helps us accept and learn from the mistakes we have made in the past. By letting go of our judgments and ending our ego-based search for perfection, we can bring our darkness to the light, dissolving anger, guilt, and shame. Piano accompaniment by Michael Gray. ISBN 1-879159-12-0 $10.00

Paul Ferrini Talks and Workshop Tapes

ANSWERING OUR OWN CALL FOR LOVE

A Sermon given at the *Pacific Church of Religious Science* in San Diego, CA November, 1997

Paul tells the story of his own spiritual awakening: his Atheist upbringing, how he began to open to the presence of God, and his connection with Jesus and the Christ Mind teaching. In a very clear, heart-felt way, Paul presents to us the spiritual path of love, acceptance, and forgiveness. 1 Cassette $10.00 ISBN 1-879159-33-3

THE ECSTATIC MOMENT

A workshop given by Paul in Los Angeles at the *Agape International Center of Truth*, May, 1997

Shows us how we can be with our pain compassionately and learn to nurture the light within ourselves, even when it appears that we are walking through darkness. Discusses subjects such as living in the present, acceptance, not fixing self or others, being with our discomfort and learning that we are lovable as we are. 1 Cassette $10.00 ISBN 1-879159-27-9

HONORING SELF AND OTHER

A Workshop at the *Pacific Church of Religious Science* in San Diego, November, 1997

Helps us understand the importance of not betraying ourselves in our relationships with others. Focuses on understanding healthy boundaries, setting limits, and saying no to others in a loving way. Real life examples include a woman who is married to a man who is chronically critical of her, and a gay man who wants to tell his judgmental parents that he has AIDS. 1 Cassette $10.00 ISBN 1-879159-34-1

SEEK FIRST THE KINGDOM

Two Sunday Messages given by Paul: the first in May, 1997 in Los Angeles at the *Agape Int'l. Center of Truth*, and the second in September, 1997 in Portland, OR at the *Unity Church*.

Discusses the words of Jesus in the Sermon on the Mount: "Seek first the kingdom and all else will be added to you." Helps us understand how we create the inner temple by learning to hold our judgments of self and other more compassionately. The love of God flows through our love and acceptance of ourselves. As we establish our connection to the divine within ourselves, we don't need to look outside of ourselves for love and acceptance. Includes fabulous music by The Agape Choir and Band. 1 Cassette $10.00 ISBN 1-879159-30-9

251

ENDING THE BETRAYAL OF THE SELF

A Workshop given by Paul at the *Learning Annex* in Toronto, April, 1997

A roadmap for integrating the opposing voices in our psyche so that we can experience our own wholeness. Delineates what our responsibility is and isn't in our relationships with others, and helps us learn to set clear, firm, but loving boundaries. Our relationships can become areas of sharing and fulfillment, rather than mutual invitations to co-dependency and self betrayal. 2 Cassettes $16.95 ISBN 1-879159-28-7

RELATIONSHIPS: CHANGING PAST PATTERNS

A Talk with Questions and Answers Given at the *Redondo Beach Church of Religious Science,* November, 1997

Begins with a Christ Mind talk describing the link between learning to love and accept ourselves and learning to love and accept others. Helps us understand how we are invested in the past and continue to replay our old relationship stories. Helps us get clear on what we want and understand how to be faithful to it. By being totally committed to ourselves, we give birth to the beloved within and also without. Includes an in-depth discussion about meditation, awareness, hearing our inner voice, and the Affinity Group Process. 2 Cassettes $16.95 ISBN 1-879159-32-5

RELATIONSHIP AS A SPIRITUAL PATH
A workshop given by Paul in Los Angeles at the *Agape Int'l. Center of Truth,* May, 1997

Explores concrete ways in which we can develop a relationship with ourselves and learn to take responsibility for our own experience, instead of blaming others for our perceived unworthiness. Also discussed: accepting our differences, the new paradigm of relationship, the myth of the perfect partner, telling our truth, compassion vs. rescuing, the unavailable partner, abandonment issues, negotiating needs, when to say no, when to stay and work on a relationship and when to leave. 2 Cassettes $16.95 ISBN 1-879159-29-5

OPENING TO CHRIST CONSCIOUSNESS
A Talk with Questions & Answers at *Unity Church,* Tustin, CA November, 1997

Begins with a Christ Mind talk giving us a clear picture of how the divine spark dwells within each of us and how we can open up to God-consciousness on a regular basis. Deals with letting go and forgiveness in our relationships with our parents, our children and our partners. A joyful, funny, and scintillating tape you will want to listen to many times. 2 Cassettes $16.95 ISBN 1-879159-31-7

Risen Christ Posters and Notecards

11" x 17" Poster
suitable for framing
ISBN 1-879159-19-8 $10.00

Set of 8
Notecards with
Envelopes
ISBN 1-879159-20-1 $10.00

Ecstatic Moment Posters and Notecards

8.5" x 11" Poster
suitable for framing
ISBN 1-879159-21-X $5.00

Set of 8 Notecards
with Envelopes
ISBN 1-879159-22-8
$10.00

HEARTWAYS PRESS ORDER FORM

Name_____

Address_____

City _____State _____Zip_____

Phone/Fax_____Email_____

BOOKS BY PAUL FERRINI

The Way of Peace Hardcover ($19.95)   _____

   Way of Peace Dice ($3.00)   _____

I am the Door Hardcover ($21.95)   _____

Reflections of the Christ Mind: The Present Day

   Teachings of Jesus Hardcover (Available April, 2000)   _____

The Seven Spiritual Laws of Relationship ($10.95)   _____

Grace Unfolding: The Art of Living A

   Surrendered Life ($9.95)   _____

Return to the Garden ($12.95)   _____

Living in the Heart ($10.95)   _____

Miracle of Love ($12.95)   _____

Crossing the Water ($9.95)   _____

Waking Up Together ($14.95)   _____

The Ecstatic Moment ($10.95)   _____

The Silence of the Heart ($14.95)   _____

Love Without Conditions ($12.00)   _____

The Wisdom of the Self ($12.00)   _____

The Twelve Steps of Forgiveness ($10.00)   _____

The Circle of Atonement ($12.00)   _____

The Bridge to Reality ($12.00)   _____

From Ego to Self ($10.00)   _____

Virtues of the Way ($7.50)   _____

The Body of Truth ($7.50)   _____

Available Light ($10.00)   _____

Audio Tapes by Paul Ferrini

The Circle of Healing ($10.00) _____
Healing the Wounded Child ($10.00) _____
Forgiveness: The Original Blessing ($10.00) _____
The Poetry of the Soul ($10.00) _____
Seek First the Kingdom ($10.00) _____
Answering Our Own Call for Love ($10.00) _____
The Ecstatic Moment ($10.00) _____
Honoring Self and Other ($10.00) _____
Love Without Conditions ($19.95) 2 tapes _____
Ending the Betrayal of the Self ($16.95) 2 tapes _____
Relationships: Changing Past Patterns ($16.95) 2 tapes _____
Relationship As a Spiritual Path ($16.95) 2 tapes _____
Opening to Christ Consciousness ($16.95) 2 tapes _____

POSTERS AND NOTECARDS

Risen Christ Poster 11"x17" ($10.00) _____
Ecstatic Moment Poster 8.5"x11" ($5.00) _____
Risen Christ Notecards 8/pkg ($10.00) _____
Ecstatic Moment Notecards 8/pkg ($10.00) _____

Shipping

($2.50 for first item, $1.00 each additional item. _____
Add additional $1.00 for first class postage _____
and an extra $1.00 for hardcover books.) _____
MA residents please add 5% sales tax. _____
Please allow 1-2 weeks for delivery   TOTAL _____

Send Order To: Heartways Press P. O. Box 99,
Greenfield, MA 01302-0099   413-774-9474
Toll free: 1-888-HARTWAY (Orders only)